Original title:
The Orchard Oracle

Copyright © 2025 Creative Arts Management OÜ
All rights reserved.

Author: Nora Sinclair
ISBN HARDBACK: 978-1-80567-060-5
ISBN PAPERBACK: 978-1-80567-140-4

The Language of Withering Petals

Petals chatter secrets in the breeze,
They gossip about the bees with ease.
Oh, the drama of the fading bloom,
Each wilt is a tale that brings the gloom.

Once vibrant hues of pink and gold,
Now they droop, and stories unfold.
A rose tells a joke, a daisy snores,
In their wrinkled laughter, life restores.

Beneath the Citrus Canopy

Under lemons, limes, and tangy oranges,
Fruitful gossip flows like gentle changes.
Lemons debate if they're sweet enough,
While oranges chuckle, 'This get's rough!'

Limes crack jokes about their zest, you see,
Citrus comedians, wild and free.
Under this canopy, laughter's contagious,
Watch out, or you may find it outrageous!

The Silence of the Grape Vine

Grape vines whisper with a cheeky grin,
Sharing last night's tale of grape juice sin.
A cabernet pranks a timid merlot,
While the pinot noir just steals the show.

In the still of night, they giggle and sway,
Plotting the next prank for the bright day.
In silence profound, hilarity brews,
Plotting their antics as the juice renews.

Signs in the Orchard's Dress

The orchard wears its signs with flair,
Bananas wearing hats as if they care.
Apples act posh, dressed in their reds,
While cherries giggle in their fruity beds.

Carrots twirl, like dancers, in grief,
Claiming they're fruits beyond belief.
In this garden of jest, all things impress,
Fashion's absurd, in their leafy dress!

Sowing Dreams in Sunlit Soil

In a garden where giggles grow,
The carrots dance, putting on a show.
Tomatoes wear hats, oh what a sight,
As radishes plot a comical flight.

In this patch of vibrant cheer,
Cucumbers gossip, oh so dear.
With every sprout a story to tell,
Seeds of laughter, oh so swell.

The Nectar of Voices Past

Banana peels slip and slide,
Old tales that fruit trees can't confide.
Apples chuckle in the breeze,
Whispering secrets with such ease.

Oranges roll with tales so bright,
Juicy gossip under the moonlight.
Lemons laugh, their zesty retorts,
In this grove of fruity cohorts.

Fables Woven in Leaf and Light

In sunny glades, the stories sprout,
Where leaves wiggle and branches shout.
Each twig a tale, each root a rhyme,
Growing giggles in perfect time.

The flowers sway in rhythm bold,
Sharing laughter that never gets old.
Wind whispers jokes through rustling trees,
A comedy show in the warm, sweet breeze.

Whispers of the Verdant Seer

Grapevines curl with clever charms,
While pumpkins flex their pumpkin arms.
The wise old oak shares puns galore,
While squirrels play chess, always wanting more.

With twinkling stars up in the sky,
The furry critters laugh and sigh.
In this realm where humor's free,
Nature's jesters hold the glee.

Visions in the Orchard's Heart

A squirrel in a bowtie, quite the sight,
Dancing with apples, morning light.
Beneath the branches, he spins and twirls,
Chasing bright shadows, a king among squirrels.

A scarecrow laughs, his clothes all askew,
Waving at crows, with a wink or two.
'Come join the party, let's sip some dew!'
And the fruit talks back, sharing gossip anew.

The Gardener's Insight

With shovel and rake, he plots a scheme,
To plant his dreams in rows that gleam.
Carrots grumble, 'This soil is too wet!'
While radishes sigh, 'We want a sunset!'

The garden gnome giggles, isn't that rich?
Eggplants whisper, 'He's in quite a pitch!'
The peas line up, for fall's grand ball,
'Let's show him how to have a good haul!'

Tales from the Gnarled Roots

Underneath the bark, secrets unfold,
A raccoon reads tales from days of old.
'Once upon a time,' he starts with glee,
'An acorn dreamt of a big oak tree!'

The roots crack jokes about growing tall,
'Last one to stretch gets no sunlight at all!'
While worms apprentice as laugh track kings,
Tickling the soil, oh what joy it brings!

Messages in the Fall

Leaves swirl down, a confetti parade,
While pumpkins plot their escapade.
'Let's trick or treat, for the fun of it!'
'Only if you promise to share the wit!'

A raccoon dressed as a ghost floats by,
With a little hat made from a ripe lemon pie.
All gather 'round, in the crisp, cool air,
For tales of mischief, without a care.

Prophecies in Petals

In the garden where gnomes giggle,
A parrot preaches with a wiggle.
Roses whisper tales of old,
To nerdy squirrels, brave and bold.

Bees argue over sweet potions,
While daisies dance in silly motions.
Each petal falls with a tiny splat,
The wise old owl just tips his hat.

Tomatoes plot their escape plans,
While carrots learn to do the can-can.
Under bright suns and moonlit beams,
Cabbages share their wildest dreams.

Beneath the Canopy of Dreams

Beneath the leaves, a dance begins,
With chipmunks wearing goofy fins.
The vines gossip beneath the skies,
About the pears and their surprise.

Cherries blush while apples chuckle,
Grapes trip over, what a shuffle!
The moon hangs low, a bright balloon,
While fairies twirl to a silly tune.

Cucumbers think they're in a race,
With zucchinis making silly face.
A chorus sings from every tree,
Come join the fun, just wait and see!

Harvesting Shadows

In the twilight, shadows mix,
The tomatoes start their bag of tricks.
Pumpkins giggle, dressed in masks,
While moonlit squash plays silly pranks.

Carrots plan a grand parade,
Underneath the leafy shade.
Radishes tell ghostly tales,
Of secret plots and autumn gales.

A scarecrow juggles with delight,
While fireflies blink in sheer surprise.
The harvest moon takes center stage,
As veggies dance and break the cage.

The Blooming Seer's Riddle

There's a bloom with a curious wink,
Telling secrets while they think.
Ferns unravel a fuzzy clue,
What's the answer? No one knew!

Petals squabble in the breeze,
Arguing who holds the keys.
A daffodil, proud and tall,
Says, "I know what's best for all!"

A cunning vine starts to plot,
To steal the show, or maybe not.
Solstice cakes and pie galore,
A real feast of whimsy to explore!

The Auditory Fruit

In the garden of giggles, fruits sing,
Whispering secrets, the vines all swing.
Apples chuckle, grapes crack a smile,
Peaches tease with a juicy style.

Under the branches, laughter does bloom,
Bananas slip, causing quite the boom.
Lemons shout jokes, they're quite zesty,
Oranges roll by, feeling all testy.

The pears hold court, they play with flair,
Jokers of the orchard, wit fills the air.
Kiwis crack puns, their jokes ripe and sweet,
As cherries join in, bouncing to the beat.

At dusk, the fruits toss tales divine,
Beneath twinkling stars, their humor will shine.
In this funny grove, where joy's in store,
One more giddy giggle, who could ask for more?

Revelations From the Grove's Shadow

In the shade of the trees, odd truths collide,
Fruits gossip, laughter, they cannot hide.
Peaches reveal, 'We're plump with delight!',
While lemons declare, 'We're tart, not polite!'

Apples whisper, 'We're the juiciest here,'
Oranges boast proudly, 'We're simply sincere!'
Beneath leafy canopies, tales unfold,
About fruit friendships that never get old.

Coconuts chuckle, all wrapped in their shroud,
While pears tease their skin, oh so proud.
The shadows of branches, where fun takes the lead,
Hiding the laughter like secrets to heed.

In every rustle, a joke in disguise,
The fruit's funny business under blue skies.
With every bright harvest, the orchard will cheer,
For who knew that laughter could grow here?

Conversations through the Leaves

In the breeze, whispers of joy arise,
Peering through branches, the laughter complies.
'Hey there, my friend!' a fig calls out loud,
While a shy little berry hides in the crowd.

Leaves swaying gently, their chatter is clear,
'Why did the fruit join the musical sphere?'
'To become a jam star!' a mango replies,
As giggles grow louder beneath sunny skies.

Walnuts debate, are they nuts or just wise?
While strawberries wink, always full of surprise.
'We're all in this together,' a fruit salad beams,
Creating wild stories from orchard dreams.

With each conversation, humor takes flight,
Under the canopy, everything feels right.
In the realm of the fruits, laughter is sly,
Who knew a hedge of greens could be so spry?

Nectar of Insights Unseen

In the trees where whispers cling,
Squirrels plot and robins sing,
Secrets drip from branches wide,
As rabbits roll, their secrets hide.

Got a knack for fruit so sweet,
Cracked my teeth on something neat,
Turns out I bit a wise old sage,
Who advised me to free the cage.

Bees buzz loud, with humor fine,
Pollen dreams in every line,
Pick a pear with laughter sweet,
Dodging worms, oh what a feat!

When the sun dips low and sly,
Even raccoons have a try,
Gather 'round, it's time to toast,
To juicy tales we love the most!

Reflections in the Orchard's Stillness

Underneath the apple tree,
A gnome whispers, 'Look at me!'
He tells jokes about his beard,
And why it's never truly feared.

The pond reflects a bouncing frog,
Who dreams to dance like a hip hop dog,
Splashing ripples, making waves,
While pondering which joke he saves.

A cloud passes, soft and round,
Hovering low, it brings a sound,
'Why did the peach stop to rest?'
'It wasn't up to the fruit test!'

As twilight falls with giggles bright,
The stars come out, a silly sight,
Each twinkle tells a fruity pun,
In the stillness, we laugh and run!

Blossoms of Prophetic Dreams

Petals sway with dreams so bold,
Each flower hides a tale untold,
A daisy knows when folks will trip,
While violets giggle, feeling hip.

The bees hold conferences at noon,
Debating which is best: jam or moon?
Their sticky votes are never clear,
But they always leave with tips and beer.

Plums gossip of a daring day,
When we'll dance in a fruit buffet,
Juggling jokes like circus clowns,
With splashes of laughter all around.

Orchard paths will lead the way,
To funny tales and munchies lay,
So pick your fruit with great delight,
And snack away till the morning light!

Shadows of the Harvest Moon

Moonlight glints on squash and vine,
As raccoons scheme with clever lines,
'Who needs a plow? We've got our paws!'
With little mischief as their cause.

The pumpkins huddle, sharing laughs,
They tell tall tales of their past gaffes,
'Remember the time we tried to roll?',
'Don't remind me, it got out of control!'

A shadow strolls, it's just a cat,
Who believes he's wise and fat,
'What's the secret to ripe success?'
'Find your warmth and wear a dress!'

In the chill of the moonlit night,
Each critter dances, feeling light,
With harvest jokes and fruit so fine,
We'll party 'neath the sleepy pine!

A Tapestry of Fruits and Fables

In a grove where apples speak,
Chasing shadows, laughter's peak.
Bananas wearing silly hats,
Debating if they're sleek or fats.

A pear named Pete begins to rhyme,
While cherries dance to upbeat chime.
"Ripe or rotten, which is fun?"
Under this tree, we're never done!

Grapes giggle as they roll about,
Voicing what they lack in clout.
"I swear I saw a plum take flight!"
Nature's circus, pure delight!

Lemons wink with zestful eyes,
As oranges plot their grand surprise.
Is it a fruit or just a jest?
In this grove, we're all the best!

The Scribe of Sap and Seed

In the shade of leafy scrolls,
Berries share their quirky goals.
"Let's write tales of juicy tales!"
As laughter echoes through the dales.

A butterfly lands, trying to write,
But scribbles end up taking flight.
"Who needs words?" a squash replies,
"Just paint with sun and watch the skies!"

Cucumbers whisper secret plots,
While radishes tie clever knots.
"Did you hear about the grape's big dream?"
The fruits all chuckle, bright and gleam.

In this garden, tales are spun,
Where laughter sprouts and puns weigh a ton.
Write your fate with fruity zeal,
As nature's pen begins to squeal!

Bellies Full with Nature's Knowledge

In a kitchen bright with colors bold,
Fruits tell secrets, stories unfold.
Peaches spill tea about last night's chat,
While mangoes boast of being fat!

Pineapples think they're royalty,
Claiming crowns with delicious glee.
"Life's a feast!" a raspberry beams,
"Pack your joy in fruity dreams!"

Tomatoes burst with laughter loud,
While veggies form a funky crowd.
"Here's to wisdom, fresh and fine!"
In this banquet, everything's divine!

Full of mirth and nature's grace,
Where every bite brings smiles to face.
A platter piled high with fun,
In this garden, life's a pun!

Luscious Reveries of the Orchard

In twilight's glow, the fruits unite,
Discussing dreams of pure delight.
"Let's throw a ball under the moon!"
While berries hum a merry tune.

A peach winks, "I can moonwalk!"
And lemons join the jiving talk.
"Who knew fruit could dance so well?"
Their laughter rings, casting a spell.

Plums spin stories of wild escapades,
While grapefruits boast of juicy parades.
"Join our feast; it's time to play!"
As night ignites their fruity fray.

In a realm of laughter's sun,
The orchard whispers, "Life is fun!"
With each delight, spirits soar,
In this grove, there's always more!

Linger Long in the Mulberry Patch

In the patch where mulberries grow,
A bird fell down, in a dramatic show.
It squawked and flapped like it owned the place,
While I just stood there, a grin on my face.

The berries popped like tiny balloons,
As squirrels danced and hummed silly tunes.
One squirrel tripped, oh what a sight,
Spinning round like it lost a fight.

With every munch of that tasty treat,
I giggled hard, barely stayed on my feet.
A berry mustache from cheek to cheek,
Turns out, I'm quite the mulberry freak.

So linger long where the laughter flows,
In the patch where the joy just never goes.
A berry feast with a side of fun,
Eating mulberries 'til we see the sun.

Shadows Dance in the Orchard Light

The shadows sway in the gentle breeze,
While apples giggle, ripe on the trees.
They whisper secrets to the bright sun,
As the dance of shadows has just begun.

A prune in the corner laughs so loud,
Wearing a hat, oh, he's so proud.
He tiptoes near, trying to sneak,
Only to slip, oh what a peak!

Down the row there's a pear so shy,
Hiding behind branches, oh me, oh my!
But when it's revealed, it bursts out in cheer,
Spinning in circles, to everyone's jeer.

So join the shadows, let laughter ignite,
In the orchard where the fun feels just right.
With fruits so bold and characters free,
It's the silliest place you'll ever see!

The Celestial Plum's Song

A plum declared it's a star tonight,
In a glow of purple, oh what a sight!
It sang a tune, all raspy and sweet,
While cherries clapped with their tiny feet.

Beneath the tree, a fig tried to dance,
Wobbling awkwardly, not missing a chance.
"Oh look at me!" it shouted with glee,
But tripped on a twig, oh, woe is me!

Grapes joined in with a conga line,
Rolling and bouncing, feeling just fine.
They laughed so hard they almost fell,
In a fruity frenzy, all's well that ends well.

As stars twinkle in the evening mist,
The plum just smiles, it can't be missed.
With a pitch so funny, and humor so strong,
It's a celestial party, come sing along!

Hushed Conversations with the Vines

The vines are talking, oh what delight,
In whispers and giggles throughout the night.
"Did you hear that? Oh, it's quite absurd!"
A cucumber snickers, "Well, that's what I heard!"

They gossip of secrets in the moon's soft glow,
While pumpkins boast of their latest show.
"I'm the biggest!" a squash did declare,
But they all just laughed, "You're quite the square!"

A tomato blushed, red as could be,
"Oh, stop your teasing, just let me be."
But the truth is, in the twilight's embrace,
These vines bring joy, laughter, and grace.

So hush your voice, and lean in with glee,
For the vines have tales, just wait and see.
With a chuckle and cheer, they spin yarns divine,
In the wonder of night, beneath the vine.

Whispers Among the Trees

In the shade where apples glow,
The squirrels plot a heist, you know.
A pear tree shakes with laughter loud,
While branches gossip, feeling proud.

A beetle claims to know it all,
Proclaims he's won the fruit ball.
But every time he takes a chance,
A gust of wind will make him dance.

Beneath the boughs, the shadows play,
With acorns rolling, come what may.
The hummingbird, so full of glee,
Swears it did find the perfect tree.

So if you listen, lean in close,
You'll hear the fruit world's lively prose.
For all who hear, let laughter churn,
In every twist, there's joy to learn.

Secrets of the Winding Grove

A rabbit with a crooked grin,
Claims he knows where the fun begins.
He hops around with sprightly cheer,
While foxes roll their eyes in jeer.

The elderberry whispers tales,
Of wine so strong it never fails.
A grapevine shakes, its laughter loud,
As berries form a giggling crowd.

The rabbit's tales just wind and weave,
But who would dare to disbelieve?
With sass and charm, they take the prize,
In every fruit, the mischief lies.

So take a stroll, and you may find,
The winding paths where quirks entwined.
The trees will hold their secrets tight,
While nature laughs into the night.

The Fruit Seer's Lament

A fig, it claims, can tell the truth,
While peaches giggle, full of youth.
The oranges argue with full zest,
While kiwis plot how they're the best.

But one sad plum, with much to rue,
Sighs, 'I've seen it all, it's true.
Those seeds of doubt just spring and grow,
While cherries sing their highs and lows.'

In every whisper, juicy tales,
Of autumn winds and timid gales.
The laughter bursts, it never fades,
Yet every seer has their shades.

So let's raise a toast to fruit so bold,
And tales of magic yet untold.
In every orchard, laughter's bright,
Where secrets hide in plain sight.

Echoes of the Ancient Boughs

An acorn rolled with such great flair,
Dared to speak with none to share.
While old oak grumbled, 'I've been here,
With roots so deep, I scoff at fear!'

Yet murmurs float through swaying leaves,
'Our rivals show up just like thieves!'
And thus began a clash of trees,
With butterfly scouts buzzing, 'Please!'

The willow swoons, dramatic grace,
Proclaiming, 'Who will win our race?'
But in the end, with laughter clear,
The cherry blossoms shed a tear.

For every bough has tales to tell,
Of silly fights where all is well.
And if you listen, you might hear,
The echoes laughing through the year.

A Cartographer of Flavor and Fate

In a land where apples sneeze,
And pears dance with the breeze.
Plums wag their tails in flight,
While cherries giggle, what a sight!

Grapes wear maps upon their skin,
Charting feasts where joy begins.
Bananas joke with rhymes so sweet,
While lemons tap their zesty feet.

Peaches toast the day with cheer,
While talking nuts lend us an ear.
Every fruit holds secrets bold,
In this garden, tales unfold.

So grab a basket, fill it high,
With laughs and flavors piled to the sky.
For in this land of fruity fate,
The joy of harvest, oh so great!

The Dance of Branch and Dream

In a grove where dreams take flight,
Branches twist in pure delight.
Apples wear their hats askew,
While oaks dance a jig just for you.

The lemons sip on sunny tea,
Making jokes about the bee.
Cherries spin a merry waltz,
While the bushes break down the walls.

Pickles joined a leafy choir,
Singing songs that never tire.
While nutty squirrels take the lead,
In a dance of every seed.

So close your eyes and take a chance,
Join the fruits in this wild dance.
For in this grove, where laughter gleams,
Reality blends with silly dreams.

The Wisdom of the Elder Tree

Beneath the wise and ancient bark,
Where roots entwine and squirrels spark.
Old apples teach the skipping tune,
While flowers gossip with the moon.

Branches crack with tales so grand,
Of fruity quests across the land.
Ripe figs share their juiciest plight,
While cacti ponder what is right.

The elder tree, with wisdom vast,
Recalls the friendships of the past.
So lean in close and lend an ear,
To fruity tales that bring you cheer!

Under the shade, let laughter grow,
As stories bloom and rivers flow.
In this haven, all is bright,
As the elder tree shares pure delight.

Twilight Tones of the Black Currant

In the twilight, whispers soar,
While black currants plan a score.
They plot to dance on vibrant nights,
With tangerines in fancy tights.

Underneath the velvet sky,
With juicy dreams, they twist and fly.
Grapefruits gleam with mischief's glow,
While pineapples steal the show.

O lemons laugh in mellow hues,
Crafting jokes with citrus clues.
As berries sneak a midnight snack,
With giggles echoing on the track.

So heed the tones of evening's light,
Where fruit friends gather, pure delight.
Join their caper, take a chance,
In the twilight's fruity dance!

The Color of Forgotten Wishes

In a grove where dreams once started,
Colors flew, but they were charted.
A purple wish was lost in thought,
As green balloons a party sought.

That orange laugh, it danced so free,
While blue juice dripped from a funny tree.
A yellow cat, with a wink and a cheer,
Said, "Come and join, there's laughter here!"

But wishes fade like old balloon,
As squirrels claim them 'neath the moon.
The colors blend, a funny mix,
Lost dreams now shared with silly tricks.

So if you find a wish to keep,
Make sure it's not too tired or cheap.
For in this grove of hues so bright,
Forgotten wishes take flight each night.

Beneath the Glistening Canopy

Beneath the leaves of shining green,
Squirrels giggle, unseen, yet keen.
A party starts with nuts and tea,
Hosted by a cheeky bumblebee.

The branches sway with tales of yore,
Of fruit that danced and begged for more.
Apple pies and a cherry fling,
A fruity fight, oh, what a fling!

Lemons laugh as they roll on by,
While oranges scheme with a sly guy.
"Catch the peach!" the cherry calls,
As juicy joy through laughter stalls.

So come beneath this jolly shade,
Where giggles bloom and pranks are made.
In every nibble, every crunch,
Find merry secrets in a lunch.

The Keeper of Sweet Secrets

In the heart of trees, there stands a gnome,
Guarding sweets like a happy tome.
He chuckles as he counts his treats,
While monkeys dance in sugar feats.

The secrets kept are sticky sweet,
With candy clouds beneath his feet.
"Don't tell the crows!" he whispers low,
"Or they will steal the candy show!"

Gumdrops tumble down the lane,
While lollipops sing in the rain.
The gnome just laughs at every taste,
For secrets here are not in haste.

So if you wander where apples bloom,
Watch for the gnome and his candy room.
He'll share a giggle, a sweet delight,
While keeping secrets, oh what a sight!

Seeds of Tomorrow's Revelations

Seeds scattered wide in playful paths,
Whispers shout amid the laughs.
Tomorrow's dreams in each small shell,
Germinate, oh what a spell!

A carrot attempts a stand-up show,
While radishes roll, full of glow.
"Plant me deep!" the pumpkin said,
As baskets tumbled with laughter spread.

Beans in jackets threw a dance,
Taking turns, they spun by chance.
Lettuce rolled with leafy grace,
Chasing shadows in the space.

So if you plant a seed today,
Watch the wonders come out to play.
For every sprout brings funny tales,
In gardens where joy never fails!

Secrets Held in Ripening Citrus

In a grove where oranges prance,
Lemons laugh and take a chance,
Grapefruits gossip with delight,
Sharing tales from day till night.

Peeling back their sunny skins,
Juicy secrets, oh the sins,
Citrus wonders, bright and bold,
Telling jokes that never get old.

Limes with zesty, cheeky grins,
Play charades with juicy twins,
Mandarin with tiny flair,
Squeezes laughter in the air.

And when the harvest comes to hand,
These fruity jesters take the stand,
For in this grove, the truth will bend,
With every laugh, the fun won't end.

The Sage Beneath the Eucalyptus

A sage tree sways with funky moves,
Spinning tales, the groove improves,
Beneath its shade, where stories flow,
Whispers dance, as breezes blow.

Kangaroos join in the fun,
With hops and skips, they've just begun,
Eucalyptus perfume in the air,
Giggles echo without a care.

Parrots squawk their riddles loud,
Making puzzles for the crowd,
Laughter rings from leaf to leaf,
A sage's wisdom, quite the chief.

And when the stars begin to twinkle,
The trees all sway and start to crinkle,
For in this place of kooky cheer,
Every night feels like a year.

A Harvest of Forgotten Dreams

In the field where wishes grow,
Dreams pop up like corn in rows,
Old hopes giggle, red and green,
Whispers of what might have been.

Scarecrows break into a dance,
Swirling round in their romance,
Tractor tunes the laughter's beat,
While sunflowers tap their feet.

Nightmares roast on autumn's fire,
S'mores of thought are our desire,
With every bite, a dream revived,
In this harvest, joy's derived.

Among the fruits of thought and cheer,
Forgotten dreams have gathered here,
So fill your basket, take your pick,
The funny tales will do the trick.

Pears of Prophetic Purity

Underneath the pear tree's shade,
Fruits of wisdom are arrayed,
Pears in whispers, secrets hail,
Tickling thoughts like a lively quail.

Prophecy hangs on branches low,
With juicy jokes that ebb and flow,
Every bite a savory dream,
Filling hearts with laughter's beam.

In a gathering of golden fruit,
Whimsical tales take sweet root,
Each pear a jest, a riddle spun,
In the orchard, oh what fun!

So pluck away, don't be shy,
Let your laughter soar and fly,
For in this grove, the wise are true,
With every laugh, your joy renews.

Fables of the Fruit-Laden Branches

Once a pear did scream for help,
It fell down, dashed like a yelp.
"Oh dear, I've lost my autumn flair!"
A bug replied, "You've got great hair!"

The apples chuckled, round and red,
"You think that's funny? Look ahead!"
And there beside the tired tree,
A worm danced wildly, full of glee.

An orange winked, 'I'm zestier!'
"Do you taste the rumor, dear?"
The fruit did giggle and agree,
"Let's plan a fruit-based jubilee!"

In the shadows, shadows lurk,
While the cherries just go berserk!
A lesson learned from all this cheer:
Laugh and roll, produce, my dear!

Garnet Hues of Possibility

A raspberry plotted, quite obscure,
To taste the world, and discover more.
"What's life without a little zest?"
The others said, "You are the best!"

A blueberry smirked, 'I'm round and bold,
With frost on my head, a sight to behold!'
"Let's blend our colors, make a pie,"
Cried a strawberry with a twinkling eye.

The grapes all sighed from their fine vine,
"Let us wine down while we intertwine!"
But a rogue banana slipped on through,
"You all are nuts, I've got the glue!"

With laughter ringing in the air,
Fruitful friendships, none could compare.
Together they sang, loud and free,
In hues of garnet, a jubilee!

An Elm's Gentle Counsel

An elm spoke softly, roots all spread,
"Don't wear that skin, it's better to shed!"
A crabapple asked, with a minimal sway,
"Will it make me funnier, in any way?"

The elm chuckled, leaves all a-twitch,
"Just be yourself, it's never a hitch!"
"Be plump and juicy, like summer's dream!
Life's not so serious; it's all a scheme!"

The walnuts nodded in solemn poses,
"With laughter's magic, joy arises."
While acorns giggled at their plight,
"Be the humor, be the light!"

Underneath the sun, seasons weave,
Nature's comedy we must believe.
The elm's advice, a timeless caress,
In this green world, let's all confess!

The Promise of the Spring Bud

In springtime's wink, the buds appeared,
Like little jokes, each one endeared.
"I'm not a flower!" a leaf proclaimed,\n"I'm here for laughs; it's all just games!"

A blossom giggled, bright and spry,
"I'm just a punchline dressed to fly!"
The bees buzzed by, in merry cheer,
"Bloom wherever you land, my dear!"

A petal turned with a cheeky grin,
"Watch out, world; my time begins!"
With every giggle, every light tease,
The garden danced in playful breeze.

In every branch, a story spun,
A promise made of joy and fun.
As spring unfolds, let laughter bloom,
For in this life, there's always room!

Tales of Ripened Wisdom

An apple dropped, oh what a clash,
A wise old pear embraced the crash.
"Don't judge the fruit by its outer skin,
For all that's sweet might hide the sin."

A banana laughed, with quite a cheer,
"Peel back the layers, my friend, no fear!"
The cherries giggled, they danced around,
In the orchard's heart, the truth was found.

So gather 'round beneath the leaves,
And share your tales, the fruit believes!
With laughter ripe and wisdom clear,
You'll find the answers hiding near.

When branches sway and winds do sing,
Remember this, oh humble thing:
Life's juiciest truths are often plain,
Like fruits that shine through sun and rain.

Beneath the Blossoms of Fate

In a patch so sweet, where mischief grows,
Two berries squabbled, as the tale goes.
"I'm the juiciest one!" the grape would shout,
While the orange rolled its eyes about.

"Beneath these blossoms, we must decide,
Who's the juiciest, what's the pride?"
The blossoms giggled, their colors bright,
"Oh, you silly fruits, don't start a fight!"

Pears tossed puns, and apples played pranks,
Laughter erupted, with joyful thanks.
The nectarines danced, with such a flair,
Reminding them all to love and share.

So if you wander where the roots entwine,
Remember that joy is the sweetest vine.
With humor and friendship, life's never late,
Just look and laugh, beneath this fate.

The Fruit Seer's Confession

A fig once claimed it saw the way,
To futures bright on a sunny day.
"Just look at me! I'm round and wise!"
But all that glitters has its lies.

A lemon piped in, with zestful cheer,
"I taste so sour, yet have no fear!"
"Don't squeeze me too tight, or I might pout,
My secrets are safe, that's what it's about!"

Peaches chimed in with giggles loud,
"We all have quirks that make us proud!"
The seer sighed, with wisdom grand,
"Before you judge, stick out your hand!"

So gather 'round, my fruity friends,
In juicy realms, the laughter blends.
For every truth has its own spin,
In the fruit bowl of life, we all can win.

Messages Carried on the Breeze

Wind whispers through the branches high,
With messages sweet as pie in the sky.
"Hey apple! You look grand today!"
"Thanks, but that worm might disagree, hey!"

A peach rolled by, with a playful grin,
"Have you heard? The figs say they can swim!"
The cactus chuckled, spiked with glee,
"Don't dive too deep or you'll miss the tea!"

Breezes flow with tales untold,
Of fruits so brave and hearts so bold.
Each gust of laughter spins a yarn,
In the patch, where no one's forlorn.

So listen close to that breezy song,
It carries wisdom, sweet and strong.
In the orchard's heart, let joy be free,
For life's best morsels are best in spree.

Nectar and Wisdom Entwined

In a garden where giggles grow,
Bees gossip tales we want to know.
Fruit falls with a plop and a thud,
Wisdom's sweet, like a fruity flood.

A squirrel steals a peach so bright,
Dancing like a silly sight.
Rabbits argue 'bout the best pie,
While birds sing nonsense in the sky.

Under the shade, laughter thrives,
With each bite, silliness arrives.
Grapes hang low, ready to tease,
Nature's jest, done with great ease.

So come, let's feast and share a laugh,
In this orchard of joy, let's take a gaffe.
With nectar sweet and humor divine,
Each fruit, a joke, in nature's design.

The Riddles of the Ripe Fig

What's round and sweet, but holds a riddle?
A fig so fine, it plays the middle.
With one bite, a squish and a squash,
Mysteries tangled, a delicious nosh.

Is it a fruit, or a trickster's prank?
Figs hide secrets like a sly prank.
They whisper softly to those who dare,
But squish too hard, and they vanish in air!

Who can solve this fruity tease?
An apple thinks it's quite the whiz.
But the fig just laughs, full of glee,
For all of us could learn its decree.

A giggle erupts from beneath the leaves,
As we ponder the fig's foolery he weaves.
In this orchard, wisdom's light,
Is found in fruit's playful bite!

The Guardian of the Gnarled Root

Beneath the trees with branches bent,
Lies a root with feelings, heaven-sent.
He guards the giggles and secrets sly,
Whispering jokes to passersby.

With curls and knots like a cheeky grin,
He's got the scoop on where to begin.
"Step lightly here!" he often croons,
"Or risk a surprise from the dancing prunes!"

From grumpy gnomes to the fairy's wink,
Life's underbelly makes you think.
This root's got stories so wild and crazy,
He'll leave you chuckling, feeling hazy.

So tip your hat as you stroll on by,
To the gnarled root with the twinkling eye.
For every laugh, beneath the sun,
His wisdom waits for everyone!

Boughs of Clarity

In the branches where antics unfold,
Life's truths wrapped in laughter bold.
Peaches giggle with a juicy jest,
Clarifying joy at nature's best.

With every swing, the fruit takes flight,
Plums joking 'bout their royal plight.
"I'm the king!" the cherries chime,
While berries burst in comical rhyme.

Underneath the canopy wide,
Laughter and wisdom coincide.
The branches sway, the wind does play,
In this orchard where we'll stay.

So grab a fruit, share a quip,
Join the feast, take a dip.
For in this place that's silly and bright,
We find our truth, wrapped in delight.

Whispers of the Gravenstein

In applesauce dreams, secrets unfold,
With laughter that ripples, stories retold.
Gravenstein giggles from branches so spry,
Winking at passersby, oh me, oh my!

A squirrel steals whispers, with nimble delight,
Claiming the fruit with a sneaky bite.
"Hey, share a slice!" the orchard trees call,
But the squirrel just chuckles, not sharing at all.

The bees are all buzzing, a comical tune,
Dancing in circles beneath the bright moon.
"Pollinate faster!" the flowers demand,
While the bees just chuckle, too busy to land.

So here in this orchard, where laughter takes flight,
Funny mishaps happen from morning 'til night.
With each ripe temptation and jest full of cheer,
The Gravenstein whispers—there's mischief right here!

Roots of Forgotten Truths

Deep down the roots, where old secrets hide,
A gopher named Gus takes the truth for a ride.
He digs up old riddles from times long ago,
Declaring them wisdom with a grand, cheesy show.

"Why did the tree cross the road?" he proclaims,
"To get to the root of its silly old games!"
The other critters just roll their small eyes,
While Gus keeps on digging for more funny lies.

A family of owls gives advice from on high,
But their wisdom gets tangled, oh my, oh my!
"With branches for wings, you can surely take flight,
But make sure to aim for the stars, not a kite!"

In a patch of green laughter, where truth gets a twist,
The roots hold the stories that can't be dismissed.
For in joyful jest, the best tales arise,
Beneath leafy shadows, with twinkles and sighs.

Insights from the Boughs

High in the boughs, the wise parrots squawk,
Sharing their gossip as they perch and talk.
"Did you hear about Betty, the peach with a tan?
She thinks she's a diva, but we know she's a fan!"

The young plums peep up and say with a grin,
"Is it true that the cherries went dancing again?
They wiggled their stems in a fruity ballet,
And left all the blossoms in utter dismay!"

Olde Maple sighs as she watches them play,
"Just don't spill the beans on this gossip today!"
But the whispers keep bouncing from leaf to bright leaf,
In this fruity world, it's the source of their grief!

So listen quite closely to tales from above,
For every small fruit has a story of love.
In the boughs of the orchard, mischief is rife,
Where laughter and joy make the essence of life!

The Call of the Apricot

Apricot calls through the sun-kissed grove,
"Come gather, you fellows, to swaddle and strove!"
With fuzzy warm hugs and a beam of bold zest,
The apricots beckon, "You're all our guest!"

The bumblebees buzz with a rhythm all their own,
"I dare you, my friend, try this ice cream cone!"
But slippery and sweet, it melts all around,
Making sticky bandits of those who surround.

The fruit flies compose a grand lively song,
While the apricot winks, "Now, what could go wrong?"
The critters all chuckle, as they twirl and they dance,
In a merry fruit riot, they seize every chance.

So heed the calls from the apricot bowl,
Where silliness reigns, and laughter takes toll.
For in every bite, there's a giggle to find,
In the orchard of joy, where we're all intertwined!

Apples of Destiny

In the garden where fruit dreams play,
A red cheeked apple rolled out one day.
It winked at the pear, gave a cheeky grin,
'Let's see who can cause the most trouble, let's begin!'

The apple climbed high, took a daring dive,
Landed right in the salad, oh, what a jive!
The salad was spiced, a mischievous thing,
And the dressing just laughed, 'Oh, now we can sing!'

A rogue fruit had joined, turning bland into fun,
'There's magic in chaos!' He shouted, 'Let's run!'
The cucumber squeaked, a small, timid shout,
But the apple just giggled, 'Let's give it a clout!'

So watch the fruits laugh, in their joyous spree,
For destiny's sweet, with a dash of glee.
In a world of greenery, they dance with delight,
Creating a feast, oh, what a silly sight!

Moonlit Branches and Fables

Under the glow of the silver moon light,
The branches whispered secrets of the night.
A squirrel with dreams of being a bard,
Wrote tales of the moon with an acorn for card.

He strummed on a twig, made the berries rejoice,
Sang ballads of apples, oh, didn't he voice!
The willow drooped low, to hear a good tale,
While the owls hooted loud, 'He shall never fail!'

A peach rolled by, and interrupted with flair,
"Your fables are sweet, but your rhythm's a scare!"
The squirrel just chuckled and gave a quick spin,
"It's laughter I'm after, let the fun times begin!"

So gather your friends, beneath branches so grand,
Where moonlight and stories create their own band.
The fables are funny, they dance through the night,
Turning whispers of laughter to pure, silly light!

The Sage Beneath the Bark

There's a wise old tree with a mustache so grand,
It tells of adventures, none can quite understand.
A worm peeks out, with a glimmering eye,
'Your tales are so tall; are they truth or a lie?'

With a creak and a groan, the tree sighed with glee,
'Oh, darling young worm, come sit here with me!
I've seen the best pranks, from hues green to red,
And once an apple danced right off my head!'

The stories resumed, of pies and of jam,
Of sneaky old owls, and the way they would scam.
In laughter they rolled, 'til the moon blinked awake,
And the worm couldn't help but giggle and shake.

So beneath all the bark, there's joy to be found,
In whispers of wisdom, and laughter resound.
For truth can wear costumes, as funny as me,
Just poke at the surface, and see what you see!

Hidden Truths of the Fragrant Soil

Beneath the surface where secrets hide,
The soil erupted with giggles inside.
With roots playing tug of war every day,
And carrots debating if they should stay!

'What's hidden down here?' asked a snicker-toned sprout,
'Is it treasure, or just worms, wriggling about?'
A radish chimed in, 'I overheard, too,
That laughter is magic, and it's growing like dew!'

The daisies above rolled their petals in cheer,
For the dirt's quick wit was all they could hear.
A sunflower stretched up, to share in the jest,
'Oh to dwell in the soil—the fun never rests!'

So next time you garden, dig deep with a spade,
For laughter in soil is a secret well played.
You'll find truths in the roots, where the funny bits bloom,

Even in dirt, you can chase away gloom!

Dreams Beneath the Canopy

Underneath the leafy shade,
A squirrel told me a joke,
He said, 'I buried my acorn,
But forgot where I woke!'

A butterfly joined in the laugh,
Flapping with glee and flair,
'You may find it,' he teased,
'If you look without a care!'

The daisies whispered cheer,
As the breeze danced around,
'Life's a riddle wrapped in fun,
Together we've found!'

And so beneath the boughs,
We spun tales with great delight,
For in this leafy enclave,
Every day felt just right!

Visions from the Garden's Heart

In the garden's vibrant glow,
A gnome reached for the sky,
He said, 'I'm planting dreams,
So I can learn to fly!'

A tomato blushed with pride,
Claiming it wore the best hat,
'I'm a veggie ripe for fashion,
Just wait 'til you see that!'

Bees buzzed a funny tune,
While flowers swayed in time,
'Let's all join the circus now,
Life's a joke in rhyme!'

And so we laughed and played,
In the garden's bright embrace,
With visions wild and wacky,
We danced in joyful grace!

Echoes Among the Apple Trees

Amidst the apple trees,
An owl gave quite a hoot,
'Why did the apple roll away?
It found its calling to loot!'

The branches shook with laughter,
As fruits began to sway,
'We're all just hanging out,'
Said an overripe pear, 'Hey!'

A rabbit twitched its ears,
With a grin wide and bright,
'Tell me more of your tales,
Or we'll stay here all night!'

So echoes filled the orchard,
With giggles on the breeze,
For among the apple trees,
Laughter tamed the trees!

The Prophecy of Falling Leaves

The leaves conspired in whispers,
'We're destined to fall soon!'
A wise old branch exclaimed,
'Let's party under the moon!'

A crunch joined in the chatter,
As the wind swirled around,
'Falling is just flying,
But with style—and ground!'

Pumpkins giggled nearby,
'We'll join the leaf parade,
With ribbons and some laughter,
In every color we've made!'

Thus the prophecy unfolded,
As night took center stage,
For in the dance of falling leaves,
Life turned a funny page!

www.ingramcontent.com/pod-product-compliance
Lightning Source LLC
Chambersburg PA
CBHW071814160426
43209CB00003B/80